THE BUILDER OF THE KABAH

Quran Stories for Little Hearts

By
SANIYASNAIN KHAN

Goodword**kidz**
Helping you build a family of faith

Long, long ago the Prophet Ibrahim ﷵ settled his wife Hajar and baby Ismail ﷵ in a lonely valley in Arabia. Thanks to the miracle of the Zamzam spring there, some people began to live there. Slowly it became a small city, which later came to be known as Makkah.

Ismail ﷺ grew up a strong and loving youth.

The Prophets Ibrahim ﷺ and Ismail ﷺ were ordered by Allah to build the House of God — the Kabah in Makkah.

build

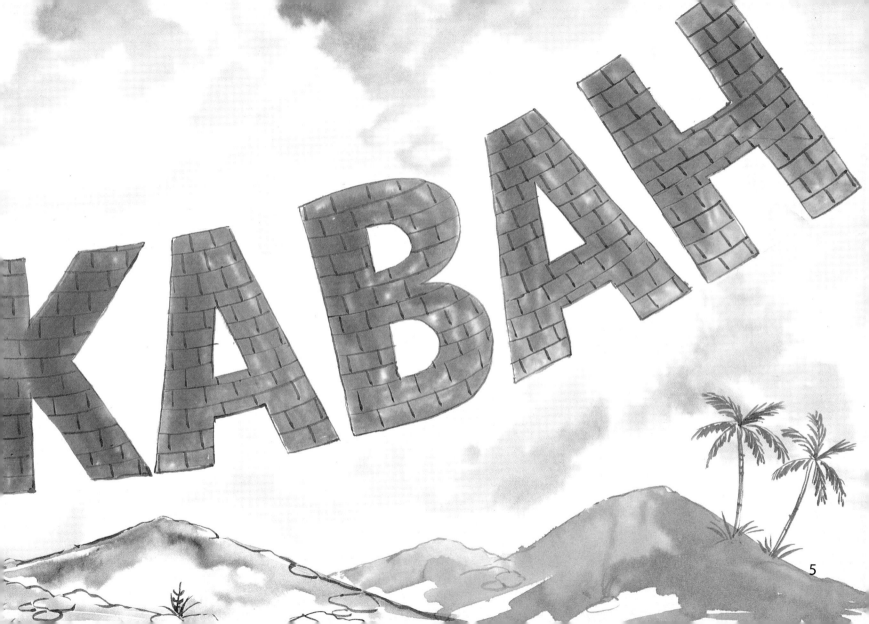

They took stones from the
nearby hills and started to work.

7

For this sacred land, Ibrahim عليه السلام prayed, "My Lord, make this land secure, and provide its people with fruits, such of them as believe in Allah and the Last Day."

As the Prophets Ibrahim ﷺ and Ismail ﷺ laid the very first stones on which the Kabah would stand, they prayed, "Our Lord, accept this from us! You are the All-hearing, the All-seeing."

They further prayed, "Our Lord, make us bow to You, and make our offspring a nation which bows to You and show us our ways of worship."

13

They also prayed for a prophet to be born in their family, who would teach wisdom to the people and purify their faith. Their prayer was answered many years later, when the Prophet Muhammad ﷺ was born to the people who came after them.

The Prophet Ibrahim عليه السلام was ordered by Allah to clean the Kabah for those who came there to pray, and to call people to Hajj.

Allah spoke thus to the Prophet Ibrahim  : "Call all people to make the Pilgrimage. They shall come to you on foot and on the backs of swift camels; they shall come from every deep ravine."

And so Allah made it a duty for all Muslims, male and female, to go on Hajj once in a lifetime, provided their means and health permitted.

Hajj is one of the five pillars of Islam. Today, over 20 million people from around the world gather in Makkah to perform this sacred duty.

The moral of the story is that believers will promise Allah to follow the example set by the Prophet Ibrahim عليه السلام and his family, doing Allah's bidding, whatever it may be, basing their lives on truth and, if necessary, giving up life's comforts and pleasures. Allah will be their focus, a goal from which they will never be turned aside by the forces of evil.

Find Out More

To know more about the message and meaning of Allah's words, look up the following parts of the Quran which tell the story of the Prophets Ibrahim عليه السلام and Ismail عليه السلام:

Surah al-Baqarah 2:125-127
Surah Al Imran 3:96-97

عليه السلام *Alayhis Salam* 'May peace be upon him.'
The customary blessings on the prophets.

ﷺ *Sallallahu alayhi wa sallam* 'May peace and Allah's blessings be on him.' The customary blessings on the Prophet Muhammad.